How to Draw

MONSTERS

For Kids

Copyright © 2020 by Tony R. Smith. All Rights Reserved. No part of this publication may be reproduced, distributed, or transmitted in any form or by any means, including photocopying, recording, or other electronic or mechanical methods, or by any information storage and retrieval system without the prior written permission of S.S. Publishing, except in the case of very brief quotations embodied in critical reviews and certain other noncommercial uses permitted by copyright law

Cylinders and Circles

CYLINDERS AND CIRCLE METHOD CAN BE USED TO CREATE ODD HEAD SHAPES LIKE MONSTERS OR ALIENS.

Example #1 Practice

Example of (Smudge Shading). Smudge Shading will give your drawing a complete look.

Example of (Tonal Shading). Tonal Shading will give your drawing a smooth contrast finish.

Example of (Hatching Shading). Hatching Shading will help blend your drawing together.

Example of (Light Smudge Shading). Light Smudge Shading will give your drawing a complete look.

1

2

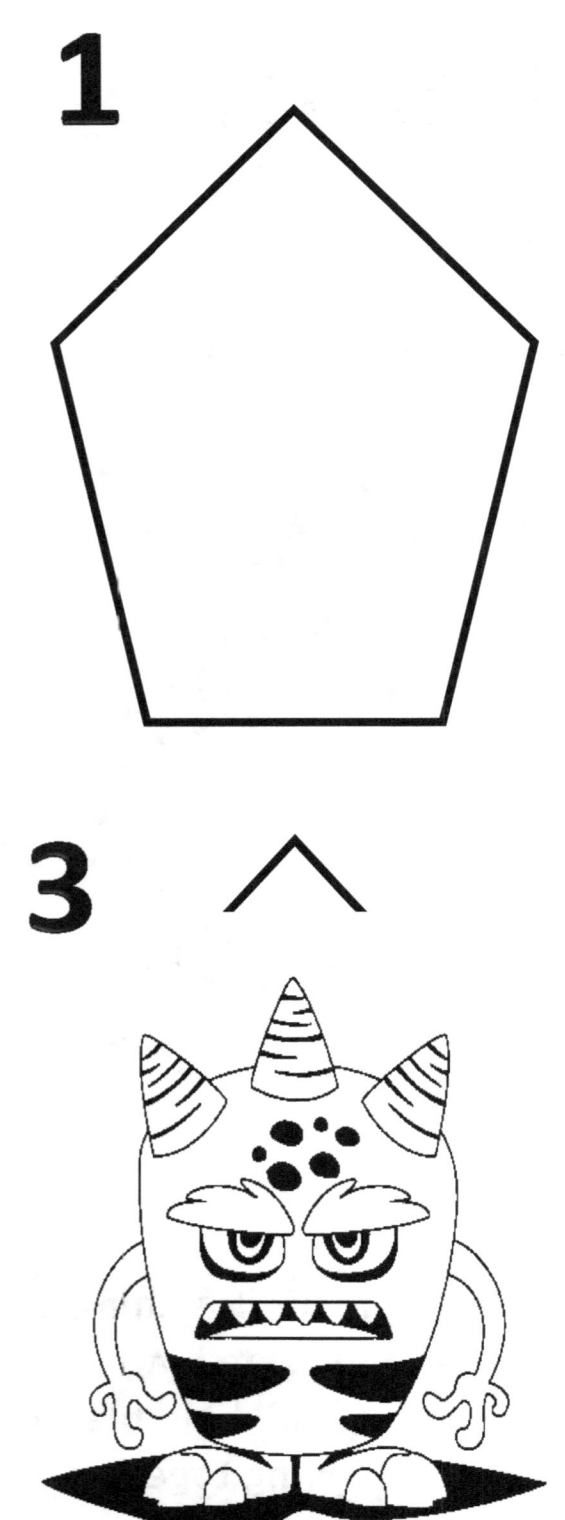

3

4

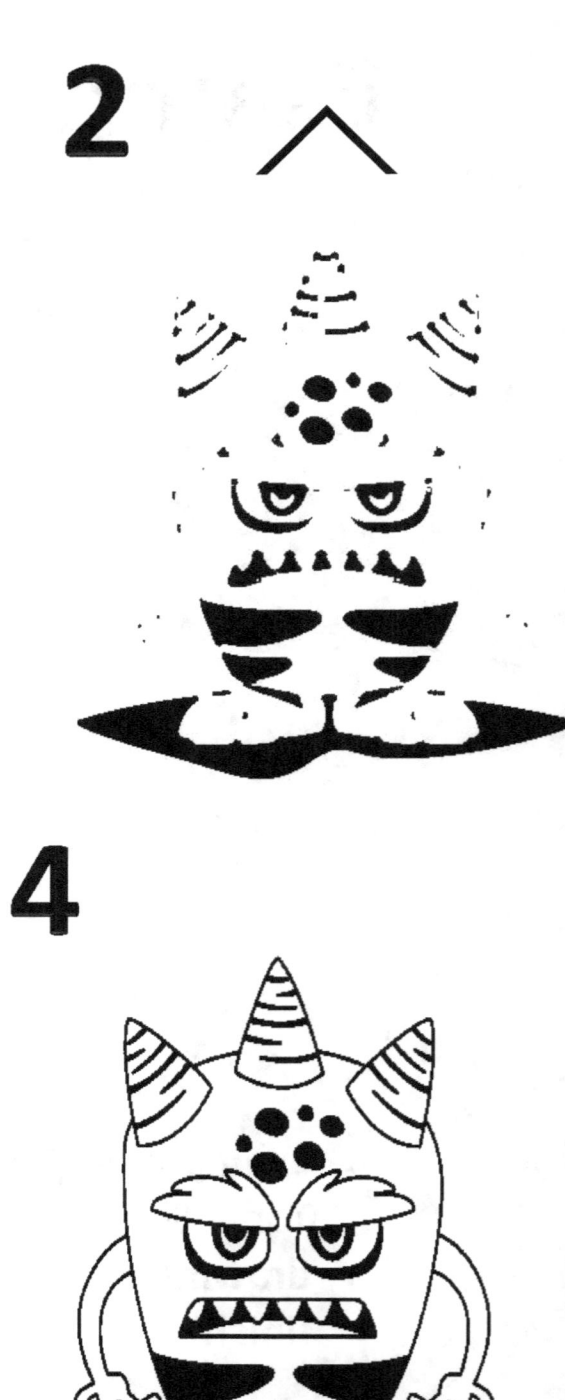

Trace the Drawing

Final Drawing

Trace the Drawing

Final Drawing

Trace the Drawing

Final Drawing

Trace the Drawing

Draw final Drawing

Trace the Drawing

Final Drawing

Trace the Drawing

Final Drawing

Trace the Drawing

Final Drawing

Trace the Drawing

Final Drawing

Trace the Drawing

Final Drawing

Trace the Drawing

Final Drawing

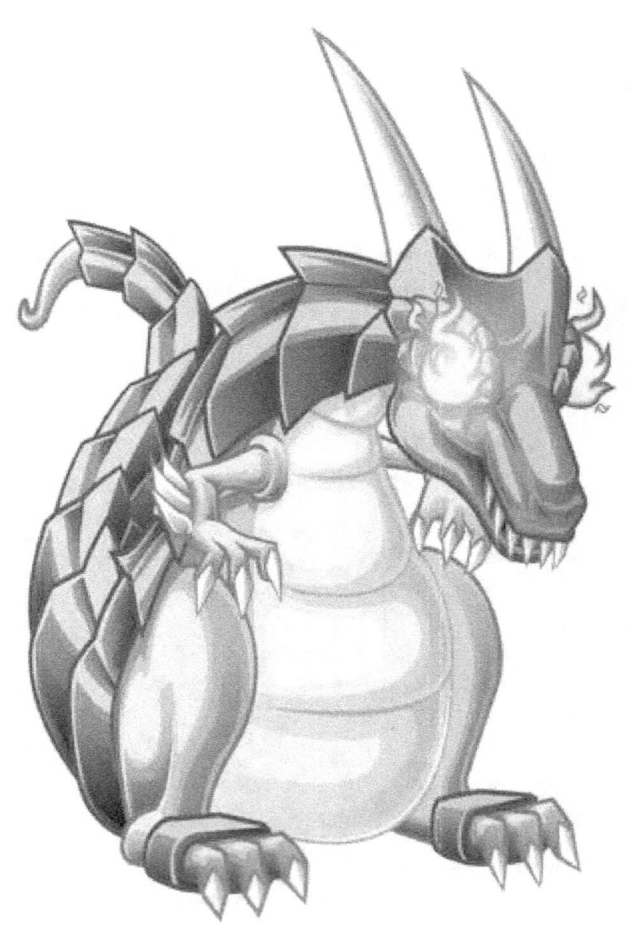

Trace the Drawing

Final Drawing

Trace the Drawing

Final Drawing

Trace the Drawing

Final Drawing

Trace the Drawing

Final Drawing

Trace the Drawing

Final Drawing

Sketch

Sketch

Sketch

Sketch

Sketch

Sketch

Sketch

Sketch

Sketch

Sketch